KU-350-833

Tips for Reading Together

Children learn best when reading is fun.

- Talk about the title and the picture on the front cover.
- Look through the pictures together so your child can see what the story is about.
- Read the story to your child, placing your finger under each word as you read.
- Read the story again and encourage your child to join in.
- Give lots of praise as your child reads with you.

Children enjoy re-reading stories and this helps to build their confidence.

Have fun!

After you have read the story,
find the bird hidden in every picture.

This book includes these useful common words:

an   got   ran   Dad

 For more hints and tips on helping your child become a successful and enthusiastic reader look at our website www.oxfordowl.co.uk.

Silly
Races

Written by Roderick Hunt
Illustrated by Alex Brychta

OXFORD
UNIVERSITY PRESS

Kipper ran.

Kipper got a banana.

Mum ran.

She got an apple.

Biff and Chip ran.

Finish

14

They got an orange.

Dad ran.

Floppy ran.

Oh no! Dad fell.

Dad got a duck!

Talk about the story

Spot the difference

Find the five differences in the two paddling pools.

Read with Biff, Chip and Kipper offers two important pathways to learning to read. **First Stories** have been specially written to provide practice in reading everyday language, and the **Phonics** stories help children practise reading by decoding sounds in words, as they learn to do in school.

Books at Level 2: Starting to read

First Stories

Phonics

Look out for the next level: Becoming a reader

First Stories

Phonics

OXFORD
UNIVERSITY PRESS

Great Clarendon Street, Oxford OX2 6DP
Text © Roderick Hunt 2007
Illustrations © Alex Brychta and Nick Schon 2007
First published 2007. This edition published 2014
Series Advisors: Kate Ruttle, Annemarie Young

British Library Cataloguing in Publication Data
available
ISBN: 978-0-19-273993-3
Printed in China by Imago
The characters in this work are the original creation of
Roderick Hunt and Alex Brychta who retain copyright
in the characters.
10 9 8 7 6 5 4 3 2 1